By the same author

Little Red Book Series

- Little Red Book of Slang-Chat Room Slang
- Little Red Book of English Vocabulary Today
- Little Red Book of Grammar Made Easy
- Little Red Book of English Proverbs
- Little Red Book of Prepositions
- Little Red Book of Idioms and Phrases
- Little Red Book of Euphemisms
- Little Red Book of Effective Speaking Skills
- Little Red Book of Modern Writing Skills
- Little Red Book of Verbal Phrases
- Little Red Book of Synonyms
- Little Red Book of Antonyms
- Little Red Book of Common Errors
- Little Red Book of Letter Writing
- Little Red Book of Perfect Written English
- Little Red Book of Essay Writing
- Little Red Book of Word Power
- Little Red Book of Spelling
- Little Red Book of Language Checklist
- Little Red Book of Word Fact
- Little Red Book: First Dictionary

A2Z Book Series

- A2Z Quiz Book
- A2Z Book of Word Origins

Others

- The Book of Fun Facts
- The Book of More Fun Facts
- The Book of Firsts and Lasts
- The Book of Virtues
- The Book of Motivation
- Read Write Right: Common Errors in English
- The Students' Companion
- Fun with Riddles
- Fun with Puzzles
- Fun with Maths

FUN WITH NUMBERS

TERRY O'BRIEN

RUPA

Published by
Rupa Publications India Pvt. Ltd 2013
7/16, Ansari Road, Daryaganj
New Delhi 110002

Sales centres:

Allahabad Bengaluru Chennai
Hyderabad Jaipur Kathmandu
Kolkata Mumbai

Copyright © Terry O'Brien 2013

While every effort has been made to trace copyright holders and obtain permission for the images used in this book, this has not been possible in all cases; any omissions brought to our attention will be remedied in future editions.

All rights reserved.
No part of this publication may be reproduced, transmitted, or stored in a retrieval system, in any form or by any means, electronic, mechanical, photocopying, recording or otherwise, without the prior permission of the publisher.

ISBN: 978-81-291-2381-7

10 9 8 7 6 5 4 3 2 1

The moral right of the author has been asserted.

Typeset in Times New Roman 10/12
by Innovative Processors, New Delhi

Printed at HT Media Ltd., Noida

This book is sold subject to the condition that it shall not, by way of trade or otherwise, be lent, resold, hired out, or otherwise circulated, without the publisher's prior consent, in any form of binding or cover other than that in which it is published.

PREFACE

Wouldn't it be good if you could easily estimate how many people were in a room! We are not talking exact answers here, but answers that are **good enough** for your life. Computers don't **understand** what you are doing. So use your brain power to **double-check** everything.

Knowing your numbers is one of the most important skills. Numbers tell us what happened, or what will happen (all things being equal). Numbers are a powerful tool for understanding the past and also the future performance. They reveal a very informative story.

Knowing numbers helps one understand that one action will have a ripple effect. More importantly, it helps us see what that effect will be. **Fun With Numbers** inspires a child's learning skills. This is a head start for a child. And most importantly, it's a whole lot of fun.

What are Numbers

- ✓ Numbers are tools of maths that help you count, label and measure.
- ✓ All numbers in mathematics are different variations of zero to 10. In addition to counting and measuring, numbers are also used as labels (cellphone numbers), for ordering (serial numbers), and for various other codes (bank accounts).
- ✓ Also, numbers can be broadly classified into different types of numbers:

Number

Amazing facts zero

1. Zero was introduced by Arabians to Europe and from there on it spread all over.
2. The rules governing the use of zero appeared for the first time in Brahmagupta's book *Brahmasputha Siddhanta*.
3. Zero was invented in India by Indian mathematicians in the 5th century and was widely used in calculations, astronomy and astrology.
4. The sum of 0 numbers is 0, and the product of 0 numbers is 1.
5. The glyph for the zero digit was written in the shape of a dot, and consequently called bindu ('dot'). The dot had been used in Greece during earlier ciphered numeral periods.

Zero:

That number which, when added to any number, leaves the latter unchanged.

Without it, modern astronomy, physics and chemistry would have been unthinkable as we know them.

Its existence in the West is probably due to the Arabs, who, having obtained it from the Hindus, passed it on to European mathematicians in the latter part of the Middle Ages.

In the English language, zero may also be called *oh, null, nil or naught*.

Zero is an even number. 0 is neither positive nor negative.

The word 'zero' came from the French word 'zéro' which comes from the Venetian 'zero', which comes from the Italian word 'zefiro' which comes from the Arabic word 'safira' meaning 'it was empty', which was later used in Sanskrit as 'úûnya', meaning void or empty.

In mathematics:

The sum of zero and a negative number is negative.

The sum of zero and a positive number is positive.

The sum of zero and zero is zero.

The sum of a positive and a negative is their difference; or, if they are equal, zero.

A positive or negative number when divided by zero is a fraction with the zero as denominator.

Zero divided by a negative or positive number is either zero or is expressed as a fraction with zero as numerator and the finite quantity as denominator.

Zero divided by zero is zero.

4 *Fun with Numbers*

Number 1

In Arithmetic: $1+1=2$

In Computer Science: $1+1=0$,

In Love: $1+1=1$!

First wedding anniversary is Paper anniversary. In modern times, it may be replaced by clocks (or gold jewellery).

First month of the year is January from Janus, the god of doorways.

January's birthstone is garnet (for constancy).

January's flower is snowdrop or carnation.

January's full moon is named 'Wolf Moon'.

Number 2

The 2nd wedding anniversary is cotton (straw or calico) anniversary. In modern times, it may be replaced by china (crockery).

The number of letters, which are the starting letter of only one country name (English) in the world: O (for Oman) and Q (for Qatar).

Iowa is the only U.S. state name starting with 2 vowels: 'I' and 'O'.

The number of the U.S. state names having 3 double letters: Mississippi and Tennessee.

The only two English words with double letters 'v' are 'revving' and 'revved'.

There are two opposite sides of almost everything in the universe: male and female, **yin and yang,** positive and negative, even and odd, north and south, east and west, black and white, right and wrong, true and false, before and after, past and future, in and out, on and off, up and down...

<u>YING</u>	<u>YANG</u>
NEGATIVE	POSITIVE
FEMALE	MALE
NIGHT	DAY
PASSIVE	ACTIVE
MOON	SUN
INTUITIVE	LOGICAL
COLD	HOT
SOFT	HARD

In the binary system, we count on our 2 fists! In the decimal system, we count on our 10 fingers.

Number 3

Third wedding anniversary is leather anniversary. In modern times, it may be replaced by crystal (or pearls, glass).

The number of colours of the regular traffic lights: green, red and yellow.

The number of rings in most popular paper binders: 3-ring binders.

The largest number of double letters in the U.S. state names: Mississippi and Tennessee.

The most popular number of wheels of an automobile is 4. The second most popular number is 3.

The number of wheels of a tricycle or a 'cyclo'.

'The 3 o'clock direction' is towards the right-hand side.

Time is divided into 3 periods: past, present and future.

The (old) popular 3.5″ photo print is of the size 3.5″×5′.

The length of a standard 'golf' wood-pencil is 3.5 inches (usually without eraser).

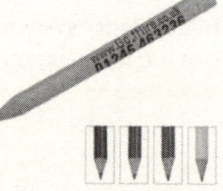

Number 4

The Fourth wedding anniversary is named fruit (or flowers, books) anniversary. In modern times, it may be replaced by appliances (or blue topaz).

The number of main lines on a palm, according to palmistry or chiromancy: life line, head line, heart line and Saturn line.

Pack of soft drink cans or bottles: 4, 6, 12, 18, 20, 24, 30 or 36.

The most popular number of wheels of an automobile is 4. The second most popular number is 3.

The popular 4″ photo print is of the size 4″×6″.

The number of the U.S. state names starting with the word 'New': New Hampshire, New Jersey, New Mexico and New York.

The number of English vowels that are on the first letter row in the English language keyboard: E, U, I and O. No vowel A.

Four Seasons is the name of a popular chain of hotels.

The number to replace the letters or word 'for' in slang English.

The maximum number of vowel (I) and of consonant (S) in a U.S. state name: Mississippi. (The only English word with one vowel (i) occurring 6 times is 'indivisibility'.)

The maximum number of letters, which can be removed from the end of an English word that is still pronounced

the same: '*queue*' and '*q*'. This is the only such word in English.

The number of popular/common English words ending with 4 letters '*dous*': hazardous, horrendous, stupendous and tremendous.

The number of fingers on each hand of Walt Disney's Mickey Mouse is incidentally four.

Number 5

A five finger discount is shoplifting.

Chanel 5, a brand of perfume, introduced by the French fashion designer Gabrielle 'Coco' Chanel, on 05 May 1921. It is the first product advertised on the United Kingdom's Channel 5.

The popular 5″ photo print is of the size 5″×7″.

'Nine to Five' is a standard working schedule for a day.

'High Five' is a popular social gesture of celebrating.

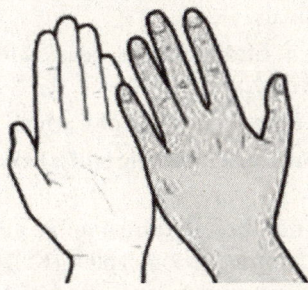

The 5th wedding anniversary is traditionally named Wood anniversary. In modern times, it can be replaced by silverware (or sapphire).

Oriental 'Five Spices' is traditionally a ground mixture of cinnamon, cloves, fennel seed, star anise and Szechuan peppercorns.

Number

Astronomy: The civil twilight is when the centre of the (refracted) Sun is 6° below the horizon.

Biology: An animal/insect has an even number of legs: 2, 4, 6, 8, 10 or more. Animals/insects having 6 legs: **flies, butterflies, moths, ants, beetles, wasps.**

Biology: A caterpillar has 16 legs before it emerges from its chrysalis to become a butterfly or moth, which has **only 6 legs.**

Biology: There might be the 6th sense, as popular belief, especially for animals.

Calendar: June's birthstone is pearl, alexandrite or moonstone (for wealth).

Chemistry: The atomic number of Carbon, C.

Chemistry: The benzene molecule is of a hexagon (regular 6-sided polygon).

Chemistry: The number of known noble gases: Helium (He), Neon (Ne), Argon (Ar), Krypton (Kr), Xenon (Xe) and Radon (Rn).

Game: The number of faces on a regular dice. Each face has one value from 1 to 6.

Geology: The number of continents on the Earth: Africa, America (North and South), Asia, Australia, Europe and Antarctica.

History: The number of years for an elected term for a Rajya Sabha M P.

Language: The shortest word in English that contains the first 6 letters A, B, C, D, E and F is *feedback*.

Language: 'Six feet under ground': dead, to be buried, the standard depth to bury a coffin.

Measure: The number of feet in a fathom, the length extended from open arm to open arm. This unit is **usually used to measure sea depth.**

Measure: The number of teaspoons in a fluid ounce.

Measure: The 6 o'clock direction is straight aback.

Money: A Maestro debit card number starts with digits 5020 or 6.

Music: The number of strings of a regular guitar.

Music: The number of holes on a standard flute.

Music: Most popular banjos have 5 strings. Other models have 4 or 6 strings.

Theology: January 6 is the Three Kings Day, the day three wise men visited the baby Jesus, which is as important as Christmas in Mexico, Puerto Rico, Spain and many Latin America countries. (Also known as Epiphany).

Trivia: The number of eggs in a carton: 6, 12, 18 or 36.

Number 7

The number of stars in the Big Dipper (Ursa Major) and also of stars in the Little Dipper (Ursa Minor).

The number of Apollo Lunar Landing missions: Apollo 11 to 17, 6 successful missions and 1 failed: Apollo 13.

The number of planets known in antiquity: Sun, Moon, Mercury, Venus, Mars, Jupiter and Saturn. And the days of the week were named after them.

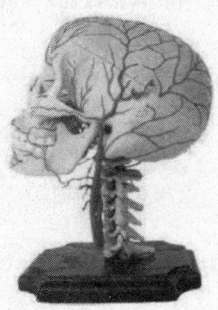

The number of neck bones (cervical vertebrae) of a human body.

The number of neck bones of a giraffe, even of its long neck.

The number of days in a week: 1 week = 7 days = 168 hours = 10,080 minutes = 604,800 seconds.

The number of 31-day months in a (solar) year: January, March, May, July, August, October and December.

September was meant the 7th month in Latin.

The atomic number of Nitrogen (N) is seven.

The 7 o'clock direction is 60° off the left-hand side to the back.

The number of dwarfs of Snow White: Bashful, Doc, Dopey, Grumpy, Happy, Sleepy and Sneezy in *Snow White and the Seven Dwarfs*.

The number of basic musical notes of major scale: C, D, E, F, G, A and B (or Do, Re, Mi, Fa, Sol, La and Ti, respectively).

The number of deadly sins: Pride, Wrath, Envy, Sloth, Lust, Gluttony and Avarice.

The number of heavenly virtues: Prudence, Temperance, justice, fortitude (which are known as the Four Natural or Cardinal Virtues) and Charity, Hope and Faith (which are known as Three Theological Virtues).

The number of days of God's Creation, according to the Holy Bible, Genesis 2:1-4: creating the whole universe and the Earth in 6 days and the 7th day was for rest.

The number of gods of light and also the number of gods of darkness in ancient Egypt.

A lucky number, according to popular belief.

14 *Fun with Numbers*

The 7ᵗʰ wedding anniversary is traditionally named copper (or wool, brass) anniversary. In modern times, it may be replaced by desk sets (or onyx).

The popular 5″ photo print is of the size 5″×7″.

7/24 or 24/7: Open 24 hours day, 7 days a week.

The number of years for a term of a French president is seven.

James Bond 007, British spy agent, a fictional movie character.

The length of a standard pencil, including the tip eraser is 7.5 inches.

Number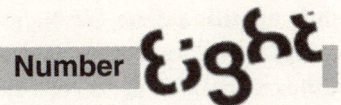

8 is a composite number, its proper divisors being 1, 2, and 4. It is twice 4 or four times 2.

A number is divisible by 8 if its last 3 digits are also divisible by 8.

8 is the base of the octal number system, which is mostly used with computers. In modern computers, a byte is a grouping of eight bits, also called an octet.

A polygon with eight sides is an octagon. Figurate numbers representing octagons (including eight) are called octagonal numbers. A polyhedron with eight faces is an octahedron.

A cube has eight vertices.

A figure 8 is the common name of a geometric shape, often used in the context of sports, such as skating.

The number eight is considered to be a lucky number in Chinese and other Asian cultures.

Hanukkah is a Jewish festival holiday that lasts eight days and eight nights.

In nuclear physics, it is the second magic number.

In particle physics, the eightfold way is used to classify sub-atomic particles.

The atomic number of oxygen is eight.

All spiders, and more generally all **arachnids**, have eight legs. Orb-weaver spiders of the cosmopolitan family Areneidae have eight similar eyes.

The octopus and its cephalopod relatives have eight arms (tentacles).

In human adult dentition there are eight teeth in each quadrant. The eighth tooth is the so-called wisdom tooth.

There are eight cervical nerves on each side in man and most mammals.

Various types of buildings are usually eight-sided (octagonal), such as single-roomed gazebos and multi-roomed pagodas.

The 8-spoked Dharmachakra represents the Noble Eightfold Path.

In Hinduism, it is the number of wealth, abundance. The Goddess Lakshmi has eight forms. There are eight *nidhi*, or seats of wealth. There are also eight Guardians of the directions.

In numerology, 8 is the number of building, and in some theories, also the number of destruction.

In astrology, Scorpio is the 8th astrological sign of the Zodiac.

An octave, the interval between two **notes with the same letter name** (where one has double the frequency of the other), is so called because there are eight notes between the two on a standard major or minor diatonic scale, including the notes themselves and without chromatic deviation.

In the 2008 Games of the XXIX Olympiad, the official opening was on 08/08/08 at 8:08:08 p.m. local time in Beijing, China.

In football, the number 8 has historically been the number of the Central Mid-fielder.

In baseball scorekeeping, the centre fielder is designated as number 8.

In rugby union, the only position without a proper name is the Number 8, a forward position.

In chess, each side has eight pawns and the board is made of 64 squares arranged in an eight by eight lattice. The eight queens puzzle is a challenge to arrange eight queens on the board so that none can capture any of the others.

A byte is eight bits.

An 'eighth' is a common measurement of marijuana, meaning an eighth of an ounce.

Referring to the shape of the numeral, eight was represented in bingo/housie slang, before political correctness, as 'One Fat Lady'. Eighty-eight was 'Two Fat Ladies'.

The numeral '8' is sometimes used in writing to represent the syllable 'ate', as in writing 'H8' for 'hate', or 'congratul8ions' for 'congratulations'.

Number NINE

There were believed to be nine major planets in the solar system. Beethoven wrote nine symphonies, and a cat is said to have nine lives.

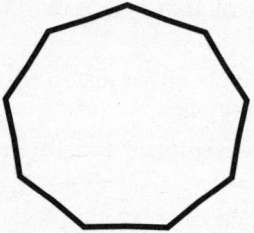

A polygon with nine angles and nine sides is called a nonagon.

In French, the word *neuf* means both *nine* and *new*.

In German, the words for nine and new are *neun* and *neu*, and in Spanish, *nueve* and *nuevo*. As you count and reach nine, you know you are about to make a new start.

Rounders and baseball are all played with teams of nine players.

A game of squash is won by scoring nine points.

Golf courses often have nine holes.

The expression '*to the nines*' means to the highest degree.

Number  10

The 10ᵗʰ wedding anniversary is traditionally named tin (or aluminum) anniversary. In modern times, it may be replaced by diamond jewellery.

Pack of cigarettes: 10 or 20.

A popular number to start a countdown: 10, 9, 8… 1, 0.

A Ten-gallon hat holds less than a gallon.

In decimal system, we count on our 10 fingers. In the binary system, we count on our 2 fists!

Number 11

Arts: The number of stars (together with a Moon) in Vincent van Gogh's famous painting *Starry Night*.

Calendar: November was meant the 9th month in Latin.

Calendar: November's birthstone is topaz or citrine (for loyalty).

November's flower is chrysanthemum.

November's full moon is named 'Beaver Moon'.

Chemistry: **The atomic number of** Sodium (Na).

Flag: The number of points on the maple leaf on Canada's national flag.

Language: The '11th hour' usually means the last hour effort/situation. As does the 23rd hour.

Language: 'Five plus Six' or 'Two plus Nine' each has 11 English letters. Hence it is an 'honest' number.

Measure: The 11 o'clock direction is 30° to the left.

The 11th wedding anniversary is called the steel anniversary. In modern times, it may be replaced by fashion jewellery (or turquoise).

The Kentucky Fried Chicken (KFC) secret handwritten recipe, developed by its founder, Colonel Harland Sanders, consists of 11 herbs and spices.

World: The number of members of the OPEC (Organization of Petroleum Exporting Countries): Algeria, Indonesia, Iran, Iraq, Kuwait, Libya, Nigeria, Qatar, Saudi Arabia, the United Arab Emirates and Venezuela. They hold 2/3 of the world's oil reserves and make 40% of world's oil production.

Number 12

Astronomy: The nautical twilight is when the centre of the (refracted) Sun is 12° below the horizon.

Biology: The number of pair of ribs on a human skeleton (24 ribs totally).

Chemistry: The atomic number of Magnesium (Mg).

Education: The number of graded classes/levels a student must attend after kindergarten to high school.

Flag: The number of stars forming a circle on the middle of the European Union flag, representing the first 12 nations (when the Union was founded on 1 November 1993): Belgium, Denmark, France, Germany, Greece, Ireland, Italy, Luxemburg, Netherlands, Portugal, Spain and United Kingdom. The newest 3 members since 1 January 1995 are: Austria, Finland and Sweden.

Flag: The number of triangular sun rays radiated from a yellow sun in the blue triangle at the upper left corner of the national flag of Namibia.

Geology: The number of countries that the Equator runs through: Ecuador, Peru, Colombia, Venezuela, Brazil, Gabon, Congo, Zaire, Tanzania, Uganda, Kenya, Indonesia.

Language: Tween (or pre-teen) refers to a child between middle childhood and adolescence, generally in the age range of 8 to 12 years old.

Theology: The number of Apostles chosen by Jesus Christ.

New York's Wall Street got its name from a 1340-foot long and 12-foot-tall wall.

The 12th wedding anniversary is silk (or fine linen) anniversary. In modern times, it may be replaced by pearls (or jade).

The number of original members of the NATO (North Atlantic Treaty Organization), founded in 1949.

The number of Olympian gods and goddesses in Greek mythology, who ruled the universe from atop Greece's Mount Olympus.

Number 13

Mathematical Number

The number 13 is the sixth prime number, and the smallest emirp (prime, which is a different prime when reversed). It is also a Fibonacci number.

> **13 facts about the number 13**
> 1. 13 is an odd number
> 2. 13 is a prime number
> 3. 13 is 50 percent of 26
> 4. 13 is a whole number
> 5. 13 is a natural number
> 6. 13 is a positive number
> 7. 13 is a two digit number
> 8. 13 is an integer
> 9. 13 is a real number
> 10. 13 is the first teen number
> 11. 13 is an unlucky number!
> 12. 13 is never a floor in a hotel the world over!
> 13. 13 finds no place in the number of months. It ends at 12.

Roman Catholicism

The apparitions of the Virgin of Fátima in 1917 were claimed to occur on the 13th day of six consecutive months.

In Catholic devotional practice, the number thirteen is also associated with Saint Anthony of Padua, since his feast day falls on June 13.

Sikhism

According to famous Sakhi (Evidence) or story of Guru Nanak Dev, when he was an accountant at the town of Sultanpur Lodhi, he was distributing grocery to people and when he gave groceries to the 13th person he stopped there because in Gurmukhi and Hindi the word 13 is called Terah, which means *yours*.

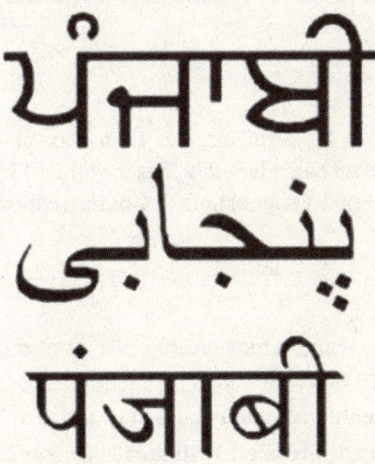

The Vaisakhi, which commemorates the creation of 'Khalsa' or pure Sikh, was celebrated on April 13 for many years.

Judaism

In Judaism, 13 signifies the age at which a boy or girl matures and becomes a Bar Mitzvah, *i.e.*, a full member of the Jewish faith (is qualified to be counted as a member of Minyan).

The Thirteen Principles of Jewish Faith

According to Rabbinic commentary on the Torah, God has 13 Attributes of Mercy.

Islam

In Shia Islam 13 signifies the 13th day of the month of Rajab (Lunar calendar), which is the birth of Imam Ali. 13 also is a total of 1 Prophet and 12 Imams in the Shia school of thought.

Others

In Mesoamerican divination, 13 is the number of important cycles of fortune/misfortune.

13 is the age that adepts usually start to learn Witchcraft.

Traditionally, there are 13 witches in a coven.

Many religions have 1 Messiah or Prophet and 12 followers for a total of 13.

unlucky·13

Triskaidekaphobia: That is the fear of number 13.

The end of the Mayan calendar's 13th Baktun is superstitiously feared as a harbinger of the apocalyptic 2012 phenomenon.

Fun with Numbers 27

It's considered to be unlucky to have thirteen guests at a table.

Friday the 13th has been considered the unluckiest day of the month.

The hangman's noose: 13 turns make a traditional hangman's noose. *Anything less would not snap a neck.*

The Last Supper: At Jesus Christ's last supper, there were thirteen people around the table, counting Christ and the twelve apostles.

Full moons: A year which contained 13 full moons instead of 12 posed problems for the monks who were in charge of the calendars.

The moon's movements: The moon moves 13 degrees around the earth every day. It takes 13 days to change from Full Moon to New Moon and 13 days to change back with 1 day Full and 1 day new to equal 28 days of the Lunar Cycle.

lucky·13

Several successful sports figures have worn the number 13. Park Ji-Sung, South-Korean footballer and mid-fielder for Manchester United wears number 13.

In Italy, 13 is also considered to be a lucky number.

Some people even have 13 tattooed onto them to represent the lucky number.

Famous American country singer and songwriter Johnny Cash first released his song called 'Number Thirteen'.

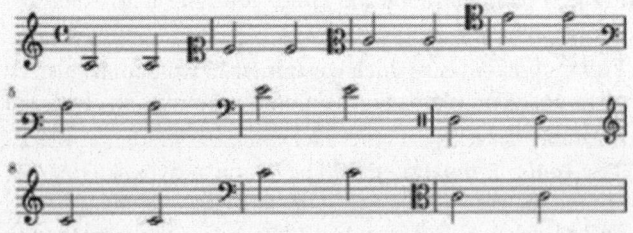

There are 13 notes, by inclusive counting, in a full chromatic musical octave.

Colgate University also considers 13 to be a lucky number. They were founded in 1819 by 13 men with 13 dollars, 13 prayers and 13 articles. In fact, the campus address is 13 Oak Drive in Hamilton, New York.

The American flag has 13 stripes in honour of the first 13 colonies.

Apollo 13 was a NASA Moon mission famous for being a 'successful failure' in that while the crew were unable to land on the Moon as planned due to a technical malfunction, they returned safely home.

FRIDAY THE 13TH

Friday the 13th is an unlucky day, and since, in this equation, each is held to be unlucky, added together, their sum can only equal double trouble.

The modern basis for the aura that surrounds Friday the 13th stems from Friday, October the 13th, 1307. On this date, the Pope of the church in Rome in conjunction with the King of France, carried out a secret death warrant against the 'Knights Templar'.

From a religious standpoint, legend has it that Adam and Eve ate the forbidden fruit, on a Friday, and later died on a Friday, and Christians consider Friday as the day on which Christ was crucified by the Romans.

The Scandinavian belief that the number 13 signified bad luck sprang from their mythological 12 demigods, who were joined by a 13th demigod, Loki, an evil cruel one, who brought upon humans great misfortune.

Triskaidekaphobia: Fear of this unlucky number
Horsemen of the Apocalypse
Number of the beast, Satan
Year of the Apocalypse, According to Mayans
Mandarin for 'not possessing'
Spiritualist, Ghostly Number
The 'Countdown to Death'
Year of the 'Curse of the Prophet'

Number 14

The number of muscles needed to smile. (43 muscles needed to frown).

The total number of phalanges (joints) of a hand (or a foot): 2 for the thumb (or the big toe) and 3 for the other 4 fingers (or 4 toes).

The number of legs of a  woodlouse.

Valentine's Day is on 14 February.

The U.S. Flag Day is on 14 June.

The number of possible types of calendar: 7 for leap years and 7 for non-leap years.

The atomic number of Silicon (Si).

The isotope Carbon-14 is used in radioactive dating of fossils.

The number of stars on the Myanmar (Burma) flag, representing 7 divisions (marked by)

The number of equal horizontal strip, alternating red

(top) and white, on the national flag of Malaysia. It also features a 14-pointed yellow star and a yellow crescent in the blue rectangle in the upper hoist-side quadrant.

The total number of special markings on a *Xiangqi* (Chinese chess) board, 5 for Soldiers (Pawns) and 2 for Cannons for each side of the 'river' at the middle of the board.

The number of letters (and spaces) available on the current version puzzle-board of the 'Wheel of Fortune' TV show: 12 each on the top row and the bottom row and 14 each on the middle 2 rows.

The US President (or Vice President) must be a US citizen over 35 years old and residing in the US for over 14 years.

The number of lines in a sonnet.

The number of days in a fortnight.

The number of digits of a credit card or ATM card number is 13 (Visa), 14 (Diners Club/Carte Blanche), 15 (American Express, JCB, enRoute) or 16 (Discover, MasterCard, Visa, JCB).

The 14th wedding anniversary is traditionally named ivory (or agate) anniversary. In modern times, it may be replaced by gold jewellery (or opal).

Number SWEET 16

The number of natural satellites of the planet Jupiter (from innermost)

The number of teeth in each jaw of a full mouth of teeth: 1 canine, 2 incisors, 2 pre-mortars (or bicuspids) and 3 mortars on each side.

The number of legs of a caterpillar before it emerges from its chrysalis to become a butterfly or moth, which has only 6 legs.

The atomic number of Sulfur (S).

The number of chess pieces for each player/side in a chess set: 8 Pawns, 2 Rooks, 2 Knights, 2 Bishops, 1 Queen and 1 King.

The smallest 2-digit square number = 4^2.

The number of feathers of a feathered shuttlecock, used in the game of badminton.

The preferred ice temperature for an ice hockey rink is 16 °F. For a figure skating ice rink, it is preferably at 22 °F.

The 16th wedding anniversary is named silver hollowware (or peridot) anniversary.

Number

Seventeen is the natural number following 16 and preceding 18. It is prime.

In spoken English, the numbers 17 and 70 are sometimes confused because they sound similar.

17 is the sum of the first four primes. 17 is the sixth Mersenne prime exponent, yielding 131071.

Seventeen is the atomic number of chlorine.

In the United Kingdom, the minimum driving age for a car or van.

In most states of the United States, Canada and in the United Kingdom, the age at which you may donate blood (without parental consent).

In many countries and regions, the age at which one may obtain a driver's license.

In the United States, the age at which one can enlist in the armed forces with parental permission.

At this age one can apply for a Private Pilot Licence (however, the applicant can start training at 16).

17 is the coming of age for wizards. It is equivalent to the usual coming of age at 18.

Described at MIT as 'the least random number', according to hackers' lore. This is supposedly because in a study where respondents were asked to choose a random number from 1 to 20, 17 was the most common choice.

The number of guns in a 17-gun salute to U.S. Army, Air Force and Marine Corps Generals, and Navy and Coast Guard Admirals.

36 Fun with Numbers

The number to call the police in France.

A slang term in the medical field for a psychiatric patient.

Number 18

Astronomy: The number of minutes between the first man, Neil Armstrong and the 2nd man, Edwin A. 'Buzz' Aldrin, landing on the Moon.

Astronomy: The number of natural satellites of the planet Saturn.

Astronomy: The astronomical twilight is when the centre of the (refracted) Sun is 18° below the horizon.

Chemistry: The atomic number of Argon (Ar).

Education: The legal age of adulthood, typical in many countries.

The 18th wedding anniversary is named porcelain (or cat's eye) anniversary.

Chemistry: The atomic number of Potassium (K).

Number 19

History: The 19-gun salute is for U.S. Vice President, Prime ministers, ambassadors and cabinet/department chiefs. Other odd-number gun salutes (17, 15, 13, 11, 7 and 5) are for lower-level chiefs. The 21-gun salute is for U.S. Presidents, chiefs of government or States or reigning royal family.

Math: A prime number. All numbers 19, 109, 1009, 10009 are prime and the next is 1000000009.

Music: The number of strings of the Vietnamese 19-stringed zither. Also, 16-stringed zither.

Sport: In golf, the clubhouse is nicknamed the 19th hole.

Sport: The score (or points) to win a ping-pong (table tennis) game or a volleyball game is 21, while the opposite player wins only 19 or less points.

Tech: The length (*cm*, centimeters) of a standard pencil, including the tip eraser.

The 19th wedding anniversary is named bronze (or aquamarine) anniversary.

The oldest age for being a teenager (13-19 years old).

Number

Biology: The number of 'baby teeth' or 'milk teeth' for a child.

Science: The minimum sound frequency (*Hz*, Hertz) that a normal human ear can hear. Normal hearing frequency range is 20-20,000 *Hz*, most sensitive 1000-4000 *Hz*.

Calendar: March 20 or 21 is the Spring Equinox day: Spring begins; day and night are equal lengths. June 20 or 21 is Summer Solstice day: Summer begins; the Sun is farthest north of the Equator.

Chemistry: The atomic number of Calcium (Ca).

Geology: The number of countries on the world having exactly one bordering country.

Measure: The number of quires in a ream of paper.

Sport: The 20-yard line in the starting line for an offensive team after a touchback in a football game.

Sport: The total regular playing time of a hockey match is 60 minutes: 3 playing periods, of 20 minutes each.

The 20th wedding anniversary is traditionally named china anniversary.

Pack of cigarettes: 10 or 20.

20: A 20-word sentence consisting of words in increasing number of letters from 1 to 20.

1. I
2. DO
3. NOT
4. KNOW
5. WHERE
6. FAMILY
7. DOCTORS
8. ACQUIRED
9. ILLEGIBLY
10. PERPLEXING
11. HANDWRITING,
12. NEVERTHELESS
13. EXTRAORDINARY
14. PHARMACEUTICAL
15. INTELLECTUALITY,
16. COUNTERBALANCING
17. INDECIPHERABILITY
18. TRANSCENDENTALIZES
19. INTERCOMMUNICATIONS
20. IMCOMPREHENSIBLENESS.

Number

Calendar: The years divisible by 100 are not leap years, unless they are also divisible by 400 in which case they are leap years, following the adoption of the current Gregorian calendar, created by Pope Gregory XIII in 1582 to reform the old Julian calendar.

Calendar: The number of years in a century. The number of decades in a millennium.

Chemistry: The atomic number of Fermium (Fm).

Game: The number of numbered letter tiles used in the game of Scrabble and 7 letters on each player's rack at a time. The board consists of 15×15 = 225 squares.

Game: Jigsaw puzzles are typically comprised of 10, 20, 50, **100**, 200, 300, 500, 750, 1000, 1500 or 2000 interlocking pieces.

History: The Hundred Years' War (1337-1453) between France and England lasted 116 years with periodic truces.

History: It is a popular saying that the Vietnamese race has **100** last names.

Language: Roman numerals: C = **100** & C-bar or (C) = 100,000.

Language: Centennial is 100 years.

Language: The minimum age to be a centenarian.

Measure: A jiffy is now standardised as 1/100 of one second or as a millisecond (*ms*).

Measure: The number of links in a chain.

1 mile = 8 furlongs = 80 chains = 5280 feet = 8000 links = 63,360 inches. Chain (or Gunter's chain or surveyor's chain) is a unit used in surveying.

Measure: The number of pounds in a hundred weight.

Measure: The number of sheets of paper in a notepad or notebook: 50, 80 or **100**.

Phone: The emergency telephone number dialing within India, Israel and Belgium.

Science: Prefixes of meaning 100: hecta-, hector- = 100.

Science: The boiling point of water: **100**°C (Celsius or centigrade) = 212°F (Fahrenheit) = 373.15 K (Kelvin).

Science: The power of 10 of a googol: 10^{100}, which is in turn the power of 10 in a googolplex: $10\wedge(10^{100})$.

Sport: The length (*m*, meters) of an international soccer field.

Sport: The standard ranges of swimming/tracking competitions (meters): 50, **100**, 200, 400, 800 and 1500. Also, for tracking: 2000, 3000, 5000 and 10000.

Sport: A standard sprint hurdle race is 110 meters for men and 100 meters for women.

Tech: Zip disks have memory capacity of 100MB, 250MB or 750MB (mega bytes) and up to 1GB or 2GB (gigabytes).

Tech: The powers of commercial incandescent light bulbs: 300W, 100W, 75W, 60W, 40W, 30W, 15W, 7.5W and 3W.

The Vatican's Swiss Guard, founded in 1506, consists of **100** volunteers who must be male, Swiss, Catholic, single, beardless and at least 5′8.

In Greek mythology, Argus is a monster with 100 eyes.

Number 999

Library: First 3 digits in Dewey Decimal Classification System call number for library books in Extraterrestrial Worlds.

Maths: Its odd powers end with 999. Its even powers end with 001.

Phone: The emergency telephone number dialing within the United Kingdom, Poland, Zambia, Uganda, Tanzania, Burma (Myanmar), Brunei, Hong Kong, Macau, Kenya, Samoa, Western Samoa, Oman, Seychelles, Uganda and Ireland.

Phone: The emergency telephone numbers dialing within Qatar are 999 and 118. The emergency telephone numbers dialing within United Arab Emirates (Abu Dhabi) are 999 and 998.

JK Rowling and Numbers

12:04AM EDT September 25, 2012: J. K. Rowling made history with her Harry Potter series, and now she's back with a dramatically different novel, *The Casual Vacancy*, her first book for adult audiences.

1997: *Harry Potter and the Philosopher's Stone*, first in the series, is published in the United Kingdom.

1998: The book is published in the U.S. as *Harry Potter and the Sorcerer's Stone*.

2007: *Harry Potter and the Deathly Hallows*, the final book in the series, is published.

450 million: Number of Potter books sold worldwide.

73: Languages in which books are available.

71: Number of times Rowling has held the No. 1 spot on USA TODAY's Best-Selling Books list.

8: Movies based on the seven-book series.

$7.7 billion: Worldwide box office of the Potter films.

2 million: Number of hardcover copies in first printing of her new novel, *The Casual Vacancy*.

Wives in History and their Numbers

King Solomon—700 Wives and 300 Concubines: The most famous polygamist is King Solomon. King Solomon had 700 wives and 300 concubines or secondary wives. Many of them were foreign princesses from lands which God had previously instructed the Israelites to avoid inter marrying.

Fatah Ali Shah Qajar—158 Wives: Fatah Ali Shah Qajar who lived from 1772 to 1834 is the second man in history with the most number of wives – 158 in all. His reign as king lasted for 37 years from 1797 to 1834. Most of his wives were princesses and he had 260 children and 786 grandchildren.

Akuku Danger—100+ Wives: The third man on the list is a prominent polygamist from Kenya. This man married more than 100 women. He was nicknamed 'Danger' because women were so attracted by his handsome looks. He married his first wife at the age of 22 in 1939 and married more than 100 wives in his lifetime and had 160 children. He divorced 85 wives for infidelity. His last marriage was in 1992.

Mohammed Bello Abubakar—86 Wives: Mohammed Bello Abubakar is another controversial polygamist from Nigeria. He married 86 wives and fathered 170 children. He claimed that he didn't seek his wives; he says his wives have sought him out because of his reputation as a healer. He worked as a preacher and Imam and lived with his family in an entire apartment block.

King David—Many Wives and Concubines: David is one of the greatest kings of Israel. According to the Bible, he was the second king of the unified Kingdom of Israel. David is a well-known polygamist having many wives and concubines although only eight wives were named in the Bible. His most famous wife is Bathsheba.

Fast Food and Numbers

Number of Fast Food Restaurants: 160,000

Number of Americans served daily: 50 Million
Annual Fast Food Revenue: $110 Billion

Frequency of fast food consumption:

Once per week	44%
Twice	20%
Three or more	14%
Seven	6%
Never	28%

Daily intake:

Percent of Daily Calories	37%
Percent of Daily Carbs	42.6%
Percent of Daily Fat	33.6%
Percent of Daily Protein	15.4%

Numbers that changed the world

3.14: Pi, formerly known as 3.14 (like Prince, but of numbers). This might be the most famous number of this millennium. Pi has an infinite number of definitions, all depending on how far you want to take it or how dorky you want to sound.

420: More accurately described as 4:20 this number will make every pothead giggle, whether it appears on a clock, a license plate, or on the take-a-number counter at the local fast food outlet.

666: If you're a math nerd, it's 3 perfect numbers in sequence. This number is even more sinister than its sister # 13. If your house number is 666, there's a 99.9% chance that it's haunted.

10,000,000,000,000,000,000,000,000,000,000, 000,000,000,000,000,000,000,000,000, 000,000,000, 000, 000, 000, 000,000,000,000,000: The inspiration for the largest data gathering service known to mankind. This number is also referred to as 'googol', which is what Google is actually named after.

365: Exactly the number of Garfield cartoons and also the number of days in a year.

10: The basis for the metric system and the most popular number of things you will find on every listing and countdown show!

Books Published in 2011 and Numbers

United States: 328,259
United Kingdom: 206,000
China: 189,295
Russian Federation: 123,336
Germany: 93,124
Spain: 86,300
India: 82,537 (21,370 in Hindi and 18,752 in English)
Japan: 78,555
Iran: 65,000
France: 63,690

The Literary World and Numbers

25 percent of all Americans believe that Sherlock Holmes was a real person.

50 copies of the Bible are sold every 1 minute. The Bible is the most shoplifted book in the world.

20 percent of all publications sold in Japan are comic books.

English author, Charles Dickens, always used to touch things 3 times for luck.

English writer William Shakespeare has zero living descendants.

Norwegian playwright Henrik Ibsen had a pet scorpion, which he used to keep on his desk for inspiration.

British writer Charles Dickens earned 0 money from his many books as he did from doing lectures.

British writer Sir Arthur Conan Doyle, the creator of Sherlock Holmes, once played cricket for the MCC and bowled to the legendary W.C. Grace.

British playwright Samuel Beckett's play *Breath* is the shortest performed play ever written. It lasts for only 35 seconds and consists of human breaths and cries.

In the 1631 publication of *The Bible*, a printer accidentally omitted the word 'Not' from the seventh commandment, encouraging readers to commit adultery.

The very first book about plastic surgery was written in 1597.

Russian writer Konstantin Mikhailov used to have 325 pseudonyms.

British writer Mary Shelly was only 19 years old when she wrote *Frankenstein*.

British writer Dr. Samuel Johnson wrote the story *Rasselas* in 1 week so he could earn the money to pay for his mother's funeral.

US writer Mark Twain's book *The Adventures Of Tom Sawyer* was the first novel to be written on a typewriter.

British poet Alfred Lord Tennyson once had 1 pony called Fanny, which used to pull his wife along in a wheelchair.

British poet Lord Byron owned 1 pet bear while he was at Cambridge University because the rules said that dogs were not allowed.

Iceland publishes more books than any other country in the world.

Scottish poet Robert Burns once owned 1 pet ewe called Poor Mallie, which he wrote two poems about.

The country with the largest number of libraries and books in the world is Russia.

The very first crossword puzzle to appear in a newspaper was in the 'New York World' in 1913.

Author John Milton who wrote the book *Paradise Lost* received just £10.00 for this classic book during his entire lifetime.

2 out of every 3 women in the world are illiterate.

There is approximately 1 library book for each and every person on earth.

Mathematicians in France produced a 400 page book showing the value of pi to one million figures.

The book *Catch 22* was originally entitled *Catch 18*.

Sir Winston Churchill wrote his book *The History of the English Speaking Peoples* when he was 82 years old.

In 1975 Indian poet Sri Chinmoy wrote 843 different poems in a single day.

Books that are made in the present day only have a life expectancy of about 100 years because the sulphuric acid in the wood pulp paper rots rapidly.

William Shakespeare's signature is worth millions of dollars. There are only 7 known specimens in the entire world.

There are more than 13,000 existing towns and cities in Great Britain that can claim to have been mentioned in the Doomsday Book.

English author Charles Dickens drew most of his inspiration from Victorian life in London. This was mainly due to the fact that he would walk as much as 20 miles a night around the streets of London to cure his insomnia.

In England in 1272 AD the cost of a Holy Bible in nine handwritten volumes cost about £33.00.

The Bible and the Numbers

1—represents absolute singleness and unity.

2—represents the truth of God's Word; for example, the law and prophets, two or three witnesses, and a sword with two edges. It is also used 21 times in the books of Daniel and Revelation.

3—represents the Godhead / Trinity. The angels cry 'Holy' three times to the triune God.

4—represents universal truth, as in the four directions (north, south, east, west) and the four winds. In acts 10:11, a sheet with four corners symbolises the gospel going to all the gentiles.

5—represents teaching. First, there are the five books of

Moses. Second, Jesus taught about the five wise virgins and used five barley loaves to feed the 5,000.

6—represents the worship of man, and is the number of man, signifying his rebellion, imperfection, works, and disobedience. It is used 273 times in the Bible.

7—represents perfection, and is the sign of God, divine worship, completions, obedience, and rest. It is used 562 times.

10—represents law and restoration. This includes the Ten Commandments.

12—represents the church and God's authority. Jesus had 12 disciples, and there were 12 tribes of Israel. The New Jerusalem city has 12 foundations, 12 gates 12 thousand furlongs, a tree with 12 kinds of fruit, 12 times a year eaten by 12 times 12,000.

40—represents a generation and times of testing. It rained for 40 days during the flood. Moses spent 40 years in the desert, as did the children of Israel. Jesus fasted for 40 days.

70—represents human leadership and judgment. Moses appointed 70 elders. The Sanhedrin was made up of 70 men. Jesus chose 70 disciples. Jesus told Peter to forgive 70 times 7.

Mythology and Numbers

0: According to some beliefs like Taoism and Buddhism it **represents spiritual emptiness and blank,** on the other hand there are some beliefs like Islam and Kabbalism, zero refers to **perfect and the symbol of limitless light and energy** and power that is boundless.

1: It is seen as the perfect completion and according to some religious orders like Hebrew it is the seat of latent intelligence and The Most High and is deemed equivalent to Adonai. It is considered as the absolute number according to the Islamic faith and Pythagoreans believe that it is the source of all things. Chinese uphold the essential masculinity of the number one. It is believed to be Yang, the celestial and auspicious power.

2: Christians believed that Christ had this duality in himself one part of him was divine and the other was human as all of us. According to Hindu beliefs, two **represents the duality of power** and Hebrews believe that it symbolises life force. Unlike one that represents the powerful part of Yin yang, two represents the other part, which is the Ying.

3: In the Buddhist traditions there are **three jewels of belief or Tri-ratna**. According to the Chinese mythology three is an auspicious number that has positive powers. Taoists believe that three is the centre point of equilibrium.

4: In Greek culture, four is the sacred number of Hermes. Jews believe that **four is the number of beneficence and intelligence.** Four also represents the four worlds of Kabbalah, for them it is memory. For Hindus four represents perfection and Brahma, one of the trinity in Hinduism is also four-faced.

5: In Christian theology five symbolises humans after their fall in the Garden of Eden. In Hindu mythology five makes the essential combinations and five also stands for severity, strength and fear. Islam believes in the five pillars, which are the five basic dogmas and Muslims pray five times a day.

6: According to Kabbalism six means beauty and creation. Christians also believe that the number is the symbol of completion and creation as God created man on the sixth day.

7: In Buddhism seven is the number of ascent and there are seven stages that one can take to transcend temporality. In Islam there are seven heavens, seven colours and seven earth and seas.

8: Buddhists believe that eight implies completion and Chinese people believe that eight means 'whole'. For

Christians eight is the number of regeneration and rebirth. Islam believes that eight are the angels who hold the reins of heaven and earth.

9: According to Hindu mythology **nine is the number of fire,** which is 'agni'.

10: It is the base of all counting and serves as the foundation of Hindu cosmology and Chinese as well.

World Towers and Numbers

International Commerce Centre
Height: 484.0 m (1,587.9 ft)
Floor count: 118

A five-star hotel, The Ritz-Carlton, Hong Kong occupies floors 102 to 118. The world's highest swimming pool and bar (OZONE) can be found on the 118th floor.

Shanghai World Financial Center

Height: 492.0 m (1,614.2 ft)
Floor count: 101

Shanghai World Financial Centre is a mixed-use skyscraper, consisting of offices, hotels, conference rooms, observation decks, and ground-floor shopping malls.

Taipei 101
Height: 508 m (1,666.7 ft)
Floor count: 101

Taipei 101 ranked officially as the world's tallest from 2004 until the opening of the BurjKhalifa in Dubai in 2010. Taipei

101 comprises 101 floors above ground and 5 floors underground. The tower is designed to withstand typhoons and earthquakes.

BusanLotte Tower
Height: 510.2 m (1,674 ft)
Floor count: 110

The BusanLotte World Tower is a 110-floor, 510.1 m (1,674 ft) supertall skyscraper project in Busan, South Korea. When built it will become the fifth tallest building in the world.

Pentominium
Height: 515.95 m (1,693 ft)
Floor count: 122

When completed, the residential tower will be 516 m (1,693 ft) tall, with 122 floors above ground.

One World Trade Centre
Height: 541.32 m (1,776 ft)
Floor count: 104

62 *Fun with Numbers*

The 104-storey supertall skyscraper is being constructed in the northwest corner of the 16-acre World Trade Center site, occupying the location where the original 8-storey 6 World Trade Centre once stood.

Mecca Royal Hotel Clock Tower
Height: 601 m (1,972 ft)
Floor count: 120

Mecca Royal Hotel Clock Tower is a building complex in Mecca, Saudi Arabia. The complex holds several world records, such as the tallest hotel in the world, the tallest clock tower in the world, the world's largest clock face, and the world's largest building floor area.

Shanghai Tower
Height: 632 m (2,073 ft)
Floor count: 121

The Shanghai Tower is a supertall skyscraper under construction in the Pudong district of Shanghai, China.

Pingan International Finance Centre
Height: 660 m (2,165 ft)
Floor count: 115

The Pingan International Finance Centre is a 115-storey supertall skyscraper that is under construction in Shenzhen, China. It is expected to be completed in 2015, and will at that time be the second-tallest building in the world, as well as the tallest in China, standing at a total of 660 m (2,165 ft) high.

BurjKhalifa

Height: 828 m (2,717 ft)

Floor count: 163

BurjKhalifa is the tallest man-made structure in the world, at 829.84 m (2,723 ft). The total cost for the project was about US$1.5 billion. The building has become the Earth's tallest freestanding structure in the Middle East where the Great Pyramid of Giza claimed this achievement for almost four millennia before being surpassed in 1311 by Lincoln Cathedral in England.

The Most Expensive Address and Number

10 Downing Street, colloquially known in the United Kingdom as 'Number 10', is the headquarters of Her Majesty's Government and the official residence and office of the First Lord of the Treasury, an office now invariably held by the Prime Minister.

Situated on Downing Street in the City of Westminster, London, Number 10 is one of the most famous addresses in the world. Over three hundred years old, the building contains about one hundred rooms.

Adjacent to St. James's Park, Number 10 is near to Buckingham Palace, the official London residence of the British Monarch, and the Palace of Westminster, the meeting place of both houses of parliament.

Originally three houses, Number 10 was offered to Sir Robert Walpole by George II in 1732.

In 1985, Prime Minister Margaret Thatcher said 'Number 10' had become 'one of the most precious jewels in the national heritage.'

Bestselling Books of all time and Numbers

1 The Holy Bible—**More than 6 Billion**

2 Mao Tse-Tung—Quotations from Chairman Mao—**900,000,000**

3 Noah Webster—The American Spelling Book—**Up to 100,000,000**

4 Mark C.—Young Guiness Book of World Records—**More than 90,000,000**

5 World Almanac Editors—World Almanac—**73,500,000**

6 William Holmes McGuffey—The McGuffey Readers—**1836 60,000,000**

7 Benjamin Spock—The Common Sense Book of Baby and Child Care—**More than 50,000,000**

8 Elbert Hubbard—A Message to Garcia—**More than 40,000,000**

9 Charles Monroe Sheldon—In His Steps, What Would Jesus Do?—**More than 30.000,000**

10 Jacqueline Susann—Valley of the Dolls—**More than 30,000,000**

Cellphone and Numbers

Mobile web experienced growth of over **700%** in the past year.

There are currently **4.1 billion** mobile phone subscriptions worldwide.

70% of installed mobile phone base is capable of browsing the Internet.

37% of consumers now reporting they own some type of Smartphone.

14.4% say they plan on buying a Smartphone in the next 90 days.

One-third of Americans (32%) have used a cell phone or Smartphone to access the internet for emailing, instant-messaging, or information-seeking.

19% of adults access the internet on a typical day with a cell or Smartphone.

One in three mobile users in France have connected to the Mobile Internet in the past 6 months with 51% connecting at least once a week.

Social media and numbers

Facebook

Monthly active users now total nearly **850 million.**

250 million photos are uploaded every day.

20% of all page views on the web are on Facebook.

425 million mobile users.

100 billion connections.

Zygna's games revenue is currently **12%** of Facebook's total income.

2.7 billion 'likes' per day.

57% of users are female.

Twitter

There are over **465 million** accounts.

175 million tweets a day.

1 million accounts are added to Twitter every day.

Top 3 countries on Twitter are USA at 107 million, Brazil 33 million and Japan at nearly 30 million.

LinkedIn

2 new members join every second.

USA leads membership at more than **57 million,** Europe has more than **34 million members.**

60% of its members live outside the USA.

In 2011, there were **4.2 billion** professionally oriented searches on the LinkedIn platform.

LinkedIn now has over **2,116 employees** (at the beginning of 2010 it had only 500).

LinkedIn is the **36th most visited website** in the world.

YouTube

3rd most visited website in the world.

2 billion views per day.

It handles **10% of the internet's traffic.**

Average YouTube user spends **900 seconds per day.**

44% of YouTube's users are aged between 12 and 34.

Over **829,000 videos** are uploaded every day.

Average video duration is **2 minutes 46 seconds.**

Google+

It was launched on **June 28, 2011.**

Google+ reached **10 million users** by July 14, 2011.

67% of Google+ users are male.

Google '+1?button is served more than **5 billion times** daily'.

It is gaining **625,000 users** per day.

Online Slang and Numbers

10-4: 'OK, Acknowledgement', as in the CB Radio 10-codes.
10x: 'Thanks'.
1337: 'Leet', short for élite, often used ironically.
143: 'I love you'.
20: 'location'; from CB Radio jargon.
224: 'today, tomorrow, forever'.
2B: 'to be'.

2B||!2B: 'to be or not to be'.
2m: 'tomorrow'.
2TM: 'to the max'.
31337: 'elite', often used ironically.
4: 'for'.
404: 'Couldn't find it', 'Clueless'.
4649: 'pleased to meet you', 'hi'.

46: 'pleased to meet you', 'hi'.

4ever, 4eva: 'forever'.

5/5: 'five by five'.

54: 'To ignore'.

666: The triple sixes sequence often represents Satan, on and of the Internet; often occurs in screennames.

8O~: Crazy, lost, drooling th desire

807, 8075: 'BOT(s)'; extreme lack of knowledge or common sense.

833r (or b33r,): beer or other alcoholic beverages.

88, 881 or 886 'bye bye': In some racist chat rooms it means 'heil Hitler', because the letter 'H' comes eighth in most Roman alphabets.

9494: 'that's it', 'that's right', 'you see?'

Bingo and Numbers

1
At the beginning/Kelly's eye
Named for the one-eyed Australian gangster called Ned Kelly

2
Me and You/One little duck
The number two is shaped like a swan

3
You and me/Cup of tea
You and me is a romantic rhyme

4
Knock at the door
One Two, buckle my shoe nursery rhyme (3 4 Knock at the door)

5
Man alive

Man alive is a simple rhyme that works here

6
Tom's Tricks/Tom Nix

Because they rhyme

7
God's in heaven/Lucky seven

As in the 7th heaven. Superstition also holds that 7 is a lucky number

8
Golden gate/Garden gate/One fat lady

Named for the shape of the number 8

9
Doctor's Orders

During World War II, the common name for the laxative pill was 'No. 9'

10
David's Den

Refers to Prime Minister David Cameron who lives at No. 10 Downing Street. When the English PM changes, the calling name also does.

11
Leg's eleven

Refers to a pair of sexy legs (2 straight up legs, side by side)

12
One dozen
Twelve is one dozen

13
Unlucky for some/Devil's number/Baker's dozen
Refers to the unlucky qualities of number 13 and the fact that 13 is a baker's dozen

14
Valentine's Day
A holiday, which falls on February 14th

15
Young and keen/Rugby team
A rugby team consists of 15 players

16

She's lovely/Sweet Sixteen

A young girl's 16th birthday is called her Sweet Sixteen

17

Often been kissed/Dancing queen

Abba's hit 'Dancing Queen' had the line 'You are the dancing queen, young and sweet, only 17'

18

Coming of age

The legal coming of age in the UK

19

Goodbye teens

Last 'teen' year before 20 comes along

20

Blind 20/One score

One score is also known as twenty

21
Key of the door
Tradition: At age 21, a child was often given a symbolic key to represent entering adulthood

22
All the twos/two little ducks
Refers to the shape of the number 2

23
She and me/The Lord is my shepherd
Refers to Psalm number 23 in the *Bible*

24
Two dozen
Self explanatory 12 plus 12

25
Duck and dive
The shape of 2 is a duck and dive rhymes with five

26
Pick and mix/Half a crown/Bed and breakfast
Traditionally, the cost of one night's accommodation plus breakfast in England used to cost '2 and 6' (two shillings and a sixpence)

27
Gateway to heaven/Little duck with crutch
Refers to the shape of the numbers

28

In a state/Overweight

Number 8 is one fat lady, but with a 2 extra it's 'overweight'

29

Rise and Shine/You're doing fine/In your prime

One more year till you are 30. You better be doing fine!

30

Blind thirty/Burlington Bertie/Dirty Gertie/Flirty Thirty/Speed Limit

Refers to the speed limit for cars in yesteryear England

31

Get up and run

No apparent reason other than it rhymes

32

Buckle my shoe

It rhymes and comes from the Rhyme, 1, 2 Buckle my shoe

33

All the threes/Dirty knees/All the feathers/Two little fleas/Sherwood forest

With both 3's here, all the 3's is a logical call. If you say 'All the trees' you will know why Sherwood Forest is used as well

34

Ask for more

Used because it rhymes

35
Jump and jive
Would appear to be for rhyming purposes only

36
Three dozen
You guessed it. A dozen is 12, 3 dozen is 36

37
A flea in heaven/More than eleven
3 is often called a flea and 7 is often used in connection with heaven

38
Christmas cake
Seems to be no reason other than rhyme

39
Steps/Those famous steps
The 39 Steps was a well known book that was adapated for film

40
Naughty forty
Popular saying that rhymes as well

41
Time for fun
Life begins at 40 is a popular saying so at 41, it is time to have fun

42

Winnie the Pooh/That famous street in Manhattan
Refers to 42nd Street in Manhattan

43

Down on your knees
Seems to be because it rhymes

44

All the fours/Droopy drawers
All the 4's is rather obvious. Droopy drawers refers to 4 looking like a pair of trousers, sagging at the waist

45

Halfway House/Halfway there
Refers to the fact that 45 is half of 90

46

Up to tricks
Only because it rhymes

47

Four and seven
It rhymes and is of course written 4 then 7

48

Four dozen
A dozen is 12. 4 times 12 is 48

49

P.C./Constable/Nick Nick
Linked to an old British radio show, PC49

50

Blind fifty/Half a century/Bull's Eye
Refers to the number of points won for a bull's eye in the game of darts

51

Tweak of the Thumb
No apparent reason other than rhyme

52

Danny la Rue/Weeks in a year
Danny la Rue was apparently a famous Drag Queen

53

Stuck in the Tree
Used because it rhymes

54

Clean the floor
No other reason other than the fact that it rhymes

55

All the fives/Snakes alive
Two 5's make it all the 5's. The shape of 5's make it snakes alive

56

Was she worth it?
This was apparently the price of an old marraige license

57

Heinz varieties
Heinz apparently had 57 varieties. Best known would be Heinz Beans

58

Choo-choo Thomas/Make them wait
58 looks a bit like a steam train and Thomas the Tank Engine was no. 8

59

Brighton Line
Traditional English bus service from London to Brighton was no. 59

60

Blind sixty/Three score/Five dozen
All are mathematical or popular calling conventions

61

Baker's Bun
Apparently only because it rhymes

62

Tickety Boo/Turn on the Screw
It rhymes, but no other apparent reason for these

63
Tickle Me
Rhyme, but no reason

64
Red Raw/The Beatle's Number
Refers to the famous song 'When I'm 64' by a band called The Beatles

65
Age old pension
Retirement age for men in England

66
Clickety Click/All the sixes
Rhyme, both sixes

67
Argumentative number/Made in Heaven
Definitely religious connotations here. 6 is bad and 7 is good

68
Saving Grace
There is a movie by that name. Any significance? None that we see

69
The same both ways/Either way up/Your place or mine/Meal for two
Six and nine can be flipped to be six and nine

70

Blind seventy/Three score and ten
A score is twenty. Three score is sixty plus ten more

71

Bang on the drum
Would appear that rhyme is the reason

72

Six dozen/Par for the course/Crutch and a duck Six times twelve (dozen)
Seven is said to look like a crutch and 2 looks like a duck

73

Queen B/A crutch and a flea
Queen B rhymes. 7 looks like a crutch and 3 looks like a flea

74

Candy store
Rhymes with the call. No other reason

75

Strive and Strive
Only because it rhymes. No other apparent reason

76

Trombones/Was she worth it?
Refers to the cost of a traditional marriage license in England that used to cost '7 and 6' (7 shillings and sixpence)

77

Sunset Strip/All the sevens/2 little crutches
Both sevens, shape of 7, 77 Sunset Strip

78

Heaven's Gate
7 is associated with heaven and eight rhymes with gate

79

One more time
This is a rhyming convention only

80

Blind 80/Eight and blank/Ghandi's breakfast
Ghandi sitting cross-legged facing his empty plate for breakfast

81

Stop and run
It rhymes, but there seems no other reason for the call

82

Straight on through/Fat lady with a duck
8 is a fat lady and 2 is a duck, the call is logical

83

Time for tea/Ethel's ear
Refers to a fat lady and the shape of an ear (3)

84

Seven dozen
7 times 12 (dozen)

85
Staying alive
Only there because it rhymes

86
Between the sticks
What sticks? Only for rhyming reasons

87
Torquay in Devon/Fat lady with a crutch
There is that fat lady again (8) with her crutch (7)

88
All the eights/Two fat ladies
Seriously, the over generously proportioned ladies (8) will be angry

89
All but one/Nearly there
Almost out of numbers, only one to go

90
Blind 90/End of the line/Top of the shop/Top of the house
The end of the numbers or the top of the list, whatever, it's logical

SMS and Numbers

The first text message was sent in **1992**

Over **70%** of mobile phone users send text messages

Text messages contribute to **20%** of operator revenues

94% of 18-24 year olds send personal texts (MDA Professional text messaging report 2003)

34% of those aged between 18-24 send 36 or more messages a week (MDA Professional text messaging report 2003)

14% of people send business text messages on their mobile phone (MDA Professional text messaging report 2003)

On New Year's Day 2003, the number of text messages sent in one day topped one hundred million for the first time, and on New Year's Day 2004, the daily total reached **111 million** messages

On New Year's Day 2005, the highest daily total ever recorded by the Mobile Data Association was reached, when **133 million messages** were sent

The Mobile Data Association predicts that **30 billion** text messages will be sent during 2005

78 million text messages were sent by Britons on

Valentine's Day 2003, 6 times more than traditional cards and a 37% increase on text figures for 2002

65 million text messages were sent throughout the UK on the last day of the 2002/3 Premiership (11th May 2003)

In December 2004, **2.4 billion** text messages were sent in Britain as the traditional Christmas card was dumped in favour of a seasonal text message

UK mobile phone owners now send **72 million** text messages on a typical day across the four UK GSM network operators

On average, **3 million** messages are sent every hour in Britain

The first local and mayoral electoral vote in the UK by text message took place on **23rd May 2002**

95% of all text messages are delivered within 10 seconds

23% of world-wide mobile users use SMS more than once a day

55% of world-wide mobile users who SMS more than once a day are 18 years old or younger

53% of Northeners use their mobile phone for sending/ receiving personal text messages

67% of women in the UK classify themselves at 'text competent' - MDA Mother's Day survey

51% of women would rather receive a text message than a card on special occasions - MDA Mother's Day survey

Who sends you personal texts? - **80% said friends/ 61% partner/ 39% parents/ 22% children** -MDA Professional text messaging report 2002

Fun with Numbers **87**

Tony Blair MP became the first UK Prime Minister to use text message technology to talk directly to the people on **25th November 2004**

The internet and numbers

#	Country or Region	Population, 2012 Est	Internet Users Year 2000	Internet Users Latest Data	Penetration (% Population)	Users % World
1	China	1,343,239,923	22,500,000	538,000,000	40.1 %	22.4 %
2	United States	313,847,465	95,354,000	245,203,319	78.1 %	10.2 %
3	India	1,205,073,612	5,000,000	137,000,000	11.4 %	5.7 %
4	Japan	127,368,088	47,080,000	101,228,736	79.5 %	4.2 %
5	Brazil	193,946,886	5,000,000	87,276,099	45.0 %	3.6 %
6	Russia	138,739,892	3,100,000	67,982,547	49.0 %	2.8 %
7	Germany	81,305,856	24,000,000	67,483,860	83.0 %	2.8 %
8	Indonesia	248,645,008	2,000,000	55,000,000	22.1 %	2.3 %
9	United Kingdom	62,698,362	15,400,000	52,731,209	84.1 %	2.2 %
10	France	65,630,692	8,500,000	52,228,905		

Books, their Titles and Numbers

One Flew Over the Cuckoo's Nest - Kesey

A Tale of Two Cities - Dickens
The Three Musketeers - Dumas
Slaughterhouse 5 - Kurt Vonnegut
The Five People You Meet in Heaven - Alborn
Catch-22 - Joseph Heller
Forty-Six Years in the Army - John McAllister Schofield
Seventy-Eight Degrees of Wisdom - Rachel Pollack
Around the World in 80 Days - Verne
100 Selected Poems - E. E. Cummings
1,000 Places to See Before You Die - Patricia Schultz
1001 Movies You Must See Before You Die - Steven Jay Schneider (Editor)

Cricketers and their Jersey Numbers

AUSTRALIANS

11 Glenn McGrath
18 Adam Gilchrist
33 Shane Watson
63 Andrew Symonds

14 Ricky Ponting
28 Matthew Hayden
58 Brett Lee

ENGLAND

11 - Andrew Flintoff
24 - Kevin Pietersen
27 - Kabir Ali
29 - Ashley Giles
32 - Alex Wharf
35 - Robert Key
38 - Vikram Solanki
69 - Owais Shah
98 - Chris Read

14 - Andrew Strauss
25 - Simon Jones
28 - Stephen Harmison
30 - Anthony McGrath
33 - Chris Tremlett
37 - Ian Blackwell
61 - Richard Johnson
78 - Ryan Sidebottom
99 - Michael Vaughan

INDIA

3 - Harbhajan
11 - Kaif
10 - Tendulkar
34 - Zaheer khan
46 - Sehwag
68 - Agarkar

7 - Dhoni
12 - Yuvraj
30 - Raina
36 - Sreesanth
56 - Irfan Pathan
99 - Ganguly

SOUTH AFRICA

3 - Jacques Kallis
6 - Justin Kemp
9 - Mark Boucher
15 - Graeme Smith
17 - AB De Villiers
27 - Jacques Rudolph
33 - Monde Zondeki
5+0 - Ashwell Prince
77 - Boeta Dippenaar
99 - Andrew Hall

06 - Herschelle Gibbs
7 - Shaun Pollock
12 - Nicky Boje
16 - Makhaya Ntini
22 - Johan Botha
29 - Johan Van Der Wath
40 - Garnett Kruger
67 - CharlLangeveldt
89 - Andre Nel

PAKISTAN

1 - Salman Butt
7 - Mohammad Sami
9 - Mushtaq Ahmed
11 - Azhar Mahmood
13 - Mohammad Yousuf
16 - Danish Kaneria
23 - Kamran Akmal
28 - Yasir Hameed
31 - Bazid Khan
88 - Iftikhar Anjum

2 - Hasan Raza
8 - Inzamam-Ul-Haq
10 - Shahid Afridi
12 - Adbul Razzaq
14 - Shoaib Akhtar
18 - Shoaib Malik
24 - RanaNaved-Ul-Hasan
30 - Arshad Khan
75 - Younis Khan
96 - Shabbir Ahmed

NEW ZEALAND

5 - C. Cumming
7 - Stephen Fleming

6 - Chris Cairns
9 - Nathan Astle

- 10 - Craig McMillan
- 12 - J Patel
- 18 - Matthew Sinclair
- 27 - Shane Bond
- 33 - James Marshall
- 37 - Kyle Mills
- 41 - Andre Adams
- 56 - Scott Styris

- 11 - Daniel Vettori
- 14 - Daryl Tuffey
- 24 - Jacob Oram
- 32 - Chris Martin
- 34 - Hamish Marshall
- 40 - Lou Vincent
- 42 - Brendon McCullum
- 70 - James Franklin

WEST INDIES

- 5 - Fidel Edwards
- 8 - Denesh Ramdin
- 13 - Sylvester Joseph
- 17 - Xavier Marshall
- 29 - Jermaine Lawson
- 33 - Daren Powell
- 38 - Tino Best
- 53 - Ramnaresh Sarwan

- 6 - Shivnarine Chanderpaul
- 9 - Brian Lara
- 15 - N Deonarine
- 23 - R Morton
- 32 - D Butler
- 34 - Ricardo Powell
- 45 - Chris Gayle
- 68 - Wavell Hinds

Numbers and Characteristics

- 1 is the most independent, unconventional, and individualistic of all numbers. It represents the beginning, the source, the innovator, the originator and the uniqueness of the individualist.
- 2 is the most gentle of all numbers, and represents cooperation, diplomacy and tact. It is a supportive number and often plays the role of advisor.
- 3 is the most playful of all numbers. It is creative, inspirational, and motivating. Self expres-sion and communication are it's central qualities. It is a happy-go-lucky number; both optimistic and enthusiastic.
- 4 is the most practical of all numbers, with a sharp eye for details. It is orderly, systematic, methodical, precise, reliable, dependable. It does what it says it will do...is honest, trustworthy, and without artifice.
- 5 is the most dynamic of all numbers. It is persuasive; a promoter and a salesperson par-excellence. It is versatile and adaptable...an experimenter and explorer. It is bright, quick-witted and a straight shooter with extraordinary reflexes. It can be easily distracted with a love for sensual pleasures and immediate gratification.
- 6 is the most loving of all numbers. It is harmonious with all other numbers, and is committed, caring, sympathetic, protective, and nurturing, as well as responsible, self-

sacrificing, and undemanding. It is domestic, marriage and family oriented and community conscious. It is the teacher and the healer.

- 7 is the most spiritual of all numbers. It is the seeker of truth, and is mental, analytical, focused, contemplative and meditative. It is the accumulator of knowledge and wisdom, and the intellectual and abstract thinker. It is insightful and understanding, self-oriented, and often withdrawn. It is the scientist, philosopher, preacher, scholar and sage.
- 8 is the most result-oriented of all numbers. It represents the balance between the material and the spiritual world. It is powerful, ambitious, and money conscious...yet generous. It understands money as a tool. It is the leader and the business person. It is understanding, forgiving, and broadminded.
- 9 is the most humanitarian of all numbers. It is effort and sacrifice without the need for reward. It is giving, sharing, loving and caring. It is the statesperson, politician, lawyer, writer, philosopher and idealist. It is worldwide consciousness, genius, and a synthesiser.

Master Numbers

These are double digit numbers such as 11 and 22. They are called Master numbers because they possess more potential than the other numbers.

- 11, for example, is the most intuitive of all numbers. It represents illumination; a channel to the subconscious; insight without rational thought; and sensitivity, nervous energy, shyness and impracticality. It's potential for growth, stability and personal power lies in it's acceptance of intuitive understanding and of spiritual truth...rather than logic alone. 11 is the psychic's number.

In Mathematics

786 is a sphenic number. 50 can be partitioned into powers of two in 786 different ways.

In Religion

The Arabic letters of the opening phrase of the Qur'an sum to the numerical value 786 in the system of Abjad numerals.

Others

786 is a United States area code in Miami-Dade County. As an overlay area code, it shares geography with other codes in order to increase the area's pool of usable numbers, bringing ten-digit dialing to the Florida Keys.

786, or Seven Eight Six, a Muslim music band

The number (when entered as ##786# or *#786#, as it is coincidentally spelling ##RUN#) is used on some Cellular Telephones to gain access to hidden menus, or to access a network monitor

Symbolism

- Discernment of the spirits, both good and evil.
- Desire, lust.
- Swift attack.
- An expression of emotion, laughing or crying.

History

Latakia, Syria is devastated by an earthquake in 555 AD. Latakia is the Biblical Laodicea, which is addressed as one of the seven churches in Revelation.

In Germany the Peace of Augsburg is established in 1555 AD to end armed conflict between the Catholic and Protestant forces in the Holy Roman Empire.

In 1555 AD Pope Marcellus II becomes the 222nd pope and is immediately followed by Pope Paul IV.

Nostradamus publishes the first version of Les Propheties (The Prophecies) in 1555 AD.

Others

In Thai, the number 5 is pronounced 'ha'. So 555 is slang for hahaha, or lol.

In Mandarin, the number sequence 555 is pronounced 'wuwuwu' (嗚嗚嗚) which is said to sound like a person crying.

In electronics, 555 is a very popular IC, which is used as a timer. It's most commonly found in an 8-pin DIP form factor.

State Express 555 is a brand of cigarettes that's very popular in Asia. They're manufactured by British American Tobacco.

The Washington Monument in Washington, DC stands at 555 feet.

555 feet is equivalent to 6,660 inches.

The U.S. telephone numbers 555-0100 through 555-0199 are reserved for fictional use while the number 555-1212 will connect to directory assitance nationally. The U.S. area code 555 is also reserved for Directory Assistance.

Fun Facts : A Medley

Common numbers and generalities in people, places, animals and other wonders

76 facts

- A hedgehog's heart beats 190 times a minute on average and drops to only 20 beats per minute during hibernation.
- An average beaver can cut down two hundred trees a year.
- An average pig squeals at a range from 100 to 115 decibels.
- An ear of corn averages 800 kernels in 16 rows.
- Average calories burned daily by the sled dogs running in Alaska's annual Iditarod race: 10,000.
- Average length of a coat hanger when straightened: 44 inches.
- Average number of eggs laid by the female American Oyster per year: 500 million. Usually only one oyster out of the bunch reaches maturity.

Fun with Numbers

- Average number of hummingbirds required to create the weight of 1 ounce: 18.
- Average number of squirts from a cow's udder needed to yield a gallon of milk: 345.
- Cats average 16 hours of sleep a day, more than any other mammal.
- During pregnancy, the average woman's uterus expands up to five hundred times its normal size.
- Every square inch of the human body has an average of 32 million bacteria on it.
- Humans shed about 600,000 particles of skin every hour - about 1.5 pounds a year. By 70 years of age, an average person will have lost 105 pounds of skin.
- If the average man never trimmed his beard, it would grow to nearly 30 feet long in his lifetime.
- In 1900 the average age of death in the US was 47.
- It takes a lobster approximately 7 years to grow to be one pound.
- On average women say 7,000 words per day. Men manage just over 2,000.
- On average, 150 couples get married in Las Vegas each day.
- On average, 42,000 balls are used and 650 matches are played at the annual Wimbledon tennis tournament.
- On average, 90% of the people that have the disease Lupus are female.
- On average, pigs live for about 15 years.
- On average, right-handed people live 9 years longer than their left-handed counterparts.

- Pregnancy in humans lasts on average about 270 days (from conception to birth).
- Smokers are likely to die on average six and a half years earlier than non-smokers.
- The ashes of the average cremated person weigh 9 pounds.
- The average adult guinea pig weighs 2 pounds.
- The average adult male ostrich, the world's largest living bird, weighs up to 345 pounds.
- The average adult raccoon weighs 21 pounds.
- The average American spends 120 hours a month watching television, the equivalent of five complete days in front of the TV.
- The average American will eat 35,000 cookies in a lifetime.
- The average American woman spends 55 minutes per day getting showered, dressed and groomed.
- The average bank teller loses about $250 every year.
- The average capacity of a pelican's pouch is 12 quarts.
- The average cat consumes about 127,750 calories a year, nearly 28 times its own weight in food and the same amount again in liquids.
- The average chicken lays about 260 eggs a year.
- The average cod deposits between 4 and 6 million eggs at a single spawning.
- The average cow produces 40 glasses of milk each day.
- The average cup of coffee contains more than 1000 different chemical components, none of which is tasted in isolation, but only as part of the overall flavour.

- The average elephant produces 50 pounds of dung each day.
- The average fox weighs 14 pounds.
- The average healthy porpoise lives 30 years.
- The average home size in the United States is now 2,200 square feet, up from 1,400 square feet in 1970, according to the National Association of Home Builders.
- The average human body contains enough iron to make a 3 inch nail, sulfur to kill all fleas on an average dog, carbon to make 900 pencils, potassium to fire a toy cannon, fat to make 7 bars of soap, phosphorous to make 2,200 match heads and water to fill a ten-gallon tank.
- The average human head weighs about eight pounds.
- The average lead pencil will draw a line 35 miles long or write approximately 50,000 English words.
- The average life expectancy of a beaver in captivity is five years.
- The average life expectancy of a kangaroo in captivity is 7 years.
- The average life expectancy of a leopard in captivity is 12 years.
- The average life expectancy of a rhinoceros in captivity is 15 years.
- The average life expectancy of geese, barring all accidents, is 25 years.
- The average life span of a mosquito is two weeks.
- The average life span of a moose is 15 to 25 years.
- The average life span of the hedgehog is 10 years.

- The average litter of Mexican wolves is between four and seven pups.
- The average llama weighs 375 pounds.
- The average mature oak tree sheds approximately 700,000 leaves in the fall.
- The average person drinks about 16,000 gallons of water in a lifetime.
- The average person falls asleep in seven minutes.
- The average person is about a quarter of an inch taller at night.
- The average person laughs about 15 times a day.
- The average person loses an average of 40 to 100 strands of hair a day.
- The average person produces 25,000 quarts of spit in a lifetime, enough to fill two swimming pools.
- The average person releases nearly a pint of intestinal gas by flatulence every day. Most is due to swallowed air. The rest is from fermentation of undigested food.
- The average person's scalp has 100,000 hairs.
- The average person uses the bathroom 6 times per day.
- The average person walks the equivalent of twice around the world in a lifetime.
- The average person's hair will grow approximately 590 inches in a lifetime.
- The average porcupine has more than 30,000 quills.
- The average porpoise weighs 103 pounds.
- The average snail moves at a rate of approximately 0.000362005 miles per hour.

- The average US male will spend 2,965 hours shaving during his lifetime.
- The FDA allows an average of 30 or more insect fragments and one or more rodent hairs per 100 grams of peanut butter.
- The linen bandages that were used to wrap Egyptian mummies averaged 1,000 yards in length.
- The size of a raindrop is around 0.5 mm - 2.5 mm, and they fall from the sky on average 21 feet per second.
- The vocabulary of the average person consists of 5,000 to 6,000 words.

- **Myth:** Police dispatch code for smoking pot is 420.

  Fact: The number 420 is not police radio code for anything, anywhere. Checks of criminal codes suggest that the origin is neither Californian nor federal.

- **Myth:** There are approximately 420 active chemicals in marijuana.

  Fact: There are approximately 315 active chemicals in marijuana. This number goes up and down depending on which plant is used.

- **Myth:** April 20th is National Pot Smokers Day.

  Fact: Well, it is now; but that wasn't the origin.

- **Myth:** April 20th is Hitler's birthday.

  Fact: Yes, it is his birthday. But, as 420 started out as a time, not a date, his birthday had nothing to do with it.

- **Myth:** April 20th is the date of the Columbine school shootings.

  Fact: This happened after the term was already in use.

- **Myth:** 4:20 is tea time for pot-smokers in Holland.

  Fact: Tea time in Holland is at 5:30 pm, or is it 2:30 pm? Seems no one is quite sure when the wonderful people of Holland drink their tea.

Marriageable age and numbers

- Algeria: 21 for males and 18 for females, lower with judicial permission if necessity or benefit is established.
- Angola: 15 with parental consent.
- Libya: 20.
- Madagascar: 18 for males, 17 for females.
- Mali: 18 or 15.
- Niger: 15.
- Afghanistan: 18 for males and 16 for females. However, more than half the marriages involve females under 16.

- Bangladesh: 21 for males and 18 for females, lunar calendar; penal sanctions for contracting under-age marriages, though such unions are not considered invalid.
- Brunei: No minimum marriage age specified.
- People's Republic of China: 22 for males, 20 for females.
- Georgia: 18, but 16 with parental consent.
- Hong Kong: 21, 16 with parental consent.
- India: 21 for males and 18 for females.
- Iran: 18 for male, 16 for female.
- Kuwait: No minimum marriage age identified.
- Maldives: According to custom, the minimum age for marriage is 15.
- Pakistan: 18 for males, 16 for females.
- Saudi Arabia: None currently, legislation for age 18 is being considered.
- Thailand: 17.

Bollywood Titles and Numbers

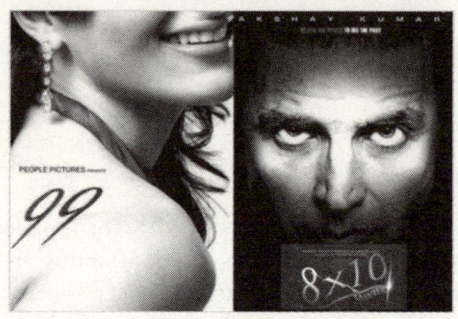

13B starring Madhavan and Neethu Chandra. As the number **13** is considered an unlucky number, the film **13B** was a spooky film.

The other films being currently on floors having numbers as titles are **99, 8×10, 611, 17, 13 and 36-24-36.**

Vikram Bhatt's supernatural film had been titled **1920.**

There had been films earlier in Bollywood that have had numerals or a combination of words and numbers: Raj Kapoor's **Shri 420** (1937), **Post Box No 999** (1958), **Victoria No 203** (1972) and VidhuVinod Chopra's **1942: A Love Story** (1994).